Wine Tasting Book for Beginners

Ultimate Wine Tasting Guide

Rebecca Thomas

Copyright

ISBN: 978-1-304-71085-7

Terms of Use

The publisher of this book and the accompanying materials have used their best efforts in preparing this book. The publisher make no representation or warranties with respect to the accuracy, applicability, fitness, or completeness of the contents of this book. The information contained in this book is strictly for educational purposes. Therefore, if you wish to apply ideas contained in this book, you are taking full responsibility for your actions.

The publisher disclaim any warranties (express or implied), merchantability, or fitness for any particular purpose. The author and publisher shall in no event be held liable to any party for any direct, indirect, punitive, special, incidental or other consequential damages arising directly or indirectly from any use of this material, which is provided "as is", and without warranties.

Contents

Brief History

In high society, wine tasting is considered a luxurious way to pass one's time when in the presence of similarly well-off company.

Nowadays, it's accepted in most any social class. Naturally, you can't just jump into wine tasting. You must first gain basic knowledge about the drink and learn how to properly taste it.

Surprisingly, wine tasting can be considered a trainable skill.

Learning about wine is simple. It comes in innumerable varieties and from locales all across the world. To measure wines against one another, you must be familiar with these numerous concoctions.

If you want to really stand out among fellow practitioners, you may also consider learning serving techniques. The contents of this e-book hope to make available to you all the pertinent information to wine tasting.

About Wine

If you didn't already know, wine is made by fermenting grapes with yeast. The yeast chemically modifies the sugars in the grapes to become alcohol.

Because of several other chemical properties of grapes, they don't require any additives for fermentation. So to speak, they naturally ferment. However, all grapes are not equal.

Generally, your output is directly affected by your input (type of grapes). If you want, you can mix several different kinds of grapes to get a unique flavor.

Wine seems to have originated around 6000 BC in Middle Eastern countries in the area of Iran, Georgia, and Israel.

Another thousand years before then, grapes and rice were being mixed together and fermented to create what serves as the ancestor of what we know today as rice wine.

European wine is much younger, only beginning circulation around 4500 BC, though the calculation of that date is heavily susceptible to human error.

Greece was among one of the earliest sites to contain traces of depictions of alcohol, and this may be where the system of crushing grapes was developed. After the discovery of wine, it gained strong footing in spiritual practices.

The ancient Egyptians often incorporated the alcoholic beverage into their ceremonial processions, and it is an integral part of mass for the Roman Catholic Church even today. Despite widespread acclaim, wine has experienced some road bumps during its large history.

At one point, it was even outright forbidden, but that sentiment faded away when distillation opened the door for therapeutic wine uses.

Types of Grapes

As we've already discussed, there are numerous "species" of grapes, each giving the wine a particular flavor. The most common variety of grape used in wines is Vitis vinifera. Using this particular grape, there are multiple possible outcomes. They are Chardonnay, Merlot, and Pinot Noir.

You're most likely to find the Vitis vinifera species growing naturally in the Rhone Valley or Bordeaux, both located in France.

That two wines are of the same vintage are not necessarily the same species. This implies that wines from the same vintage can also be created from a mixture of multiple species of grapes.

This process ends in what is known as hybrid wines. One such example is Concord grape can be bred from a wide array of grape species, as follows: Vitis labrusca, Vitis rupestris, Vitis aestivalis, Vitis riparia, and Vitis rotundiafolia.

They're primarily grown in North America and are likely the variety you'll find for sale at the market.

These types of grapes are also what you can expect to find in secondary products such as juices and jellies.

How Wine is Classified

Different regions have different systems for grouping different wines. Based on that sentence alone, there's a lot of differentiation to be expected! Many of these differences are on account of government regulations meant to both inform and protect consumers.

The European system of classification is region-based; that is, wines imported from other countries are labeled as such.

Most other non-European countries prefer to classify wines based on physical properties. That is, what kinds of grapes went into the production of the wine.

The Merlot and Pinot Noir discussed earlier are two wines that fermented using different grapes.

Although Europe seemed to initially be a minority in terms of the methodology of their wine classification, more and more are we seeing other countries adopt systems based on region rather than the species of grape.

This system has been expanded on to include not just the name of the country, but the name of the vineyard as well. Some of those locations include Napa Valley, Willamette Valley, Barrosa Valley, and Marlborough.

The least popular of the classification systems was used periodically by non-European valley regions and organized wines based on their quality.

Each attempt to implement the system has been met with poor reception.

Vintage Wine

Grapes for vintage wines are harvested and fermented with the explicit purpose of being preserved for long periods of time. Because they are circulated once a year, the flavor and color can differ across vintages.

Vintage wines are especially popular among connoisseurs who wish to preserve their wines either to increase market value or to pass down indefinitely throughout the generations. Most collectors, however, hope to drink their vintage wine during their lifetime, and preserve them only until special occasions.

Non-Vintage Wine

Non-vintage wines are produced by companies who have no interest in annually fermenting grapes from the same generation. Because they're more formulaic in their concoction, they tend to maintain consistent flavors throughout the years of their production.

For this reason, they also tend to sell in higher volume.

Flavors of Wine

Fruit Wine

If you ever see fruit wine sold at your local alcohol supply store, you'd be wrong to think grapes had any part in the process of creating them.

These wines are fermented from the fruits contained in their name. Plum wine, peach wine, apple wine…regardless the flavor, it will be explicitly stated on the packaging, especially if it's not a grape product.

Despite not being made with grapes, these drinks can be considered wines because fermentation was still required.

One of the most appealing qualities about fruit wines is that anyone can make one so long as they have sufficiently sweet fruits at their disposal in addition to sweeteners to insure there is enough sucrose for the proper chemical reactions to occur.

Other substances that can elicit fermentation reactions are citric and malic acid.

If you think back to the beginning of this book, rice wine was one of the first flavors discussed. Some people would consider it a fruit wine as well, but it more readily falls in its own category.

Nonetheless, fruit wine can be created from other non-fruit sources such as flowers so long as they are sweet enough.

Apple wine originated in Germany and, like its name suggests, is a fruit wine made from apples.

Its original German name is Apfelwein, and it contains anywhere from 5.5% to 7% of alcohol.

Unlike most other wines that have a sweet taste, Apfelwein tends to be slightly to mildly sour. Another dissimilarity it has from other wines is that it typically is sold in jugs rather than bottles.

German apple wine has become popular in American culture, making its appearance as the non-alcoholic apple cider and commonly consumed around the Thanksgiving and Christmas holiday.

You should try to consume any fruit wine product within a year of the date of purchase.

This owes to the fact that they don't age nearly as well as other wines – if they even age at all.

Their lack of aging potential is derived from additive sugars used during the fermentation process. Unlike natural fruit sugars, they can't age well.

While you can make fruit wine with virtually any fruit, the following have the best results:

Elderberries, plums, peaches, blackberries, huckleberries, blackcurrants, and pomegranates.

Those listed tend to have qualities and flavors peculiarly close to those of grape wines.

In rare cases, vegetables have also been used to ferment fruit wine, but they're not nearly as popular.

Rice Wines – Starch

Rice wine, known to the Japanese as sake, has garnered quite a reputation in the states.

In Japan, it is the most popular alcoholic beverage. Whereas grape wine is made by fermenting naturally sweet grapes, rice wine is made by fermenting the starch in rice.

The starch is converted into sugars in a process similar to that used to brew beer. Many rice wine products are diluted with water before being bottled.

Rice wine has spread from Japan to many other Asian countries such as Malaysia, Tibet, and Sabah, each with their own variety of the drinks.

Barley Wine

Barley wine originated in the 19th century. As it is actually a beer, barley wine is not to be confused as holding up to its name.

Many have fallen prey to simple misconception because of the strange name choice of the product.

Pinot Noir

All pinot noir is fermented from the Vitis vinifera grape most commonly found in the Mediterranean area and select European countries.

Although its name is name is French for black pine, this variety of grape is used primarily for red wine. Its name instead arises from the fact that the grapes on a vine cluster together in the shape of pinecones.

The fine quality of wine produced from these grapes is offset by their difficulty to cultivate. It may also be this difficulty, and implied rarity, that grants it consideration as a romantic wine.

There is deep contrast between the light color and the aroma, which closely resembles that of black cherries. The color of pinot noir can be modified though; younger grapes produce lighter colors while older grapes produce darker ones.

Chardonnay

For the first time, we'll discuss a grape that doesn't produce a dark-colored wine. Chardonnay is fermented from any variety of green grapes.

Obviously, this produces a markedly different flavor, less intense than that of its red counterpart, and referred to as a neutral wine because of it. Generally, the flavor of Chardonnay is either terroir or oak.

Chardonnay also has the distinction of being present in many forms from dry and still to sweet harvest. A second factor that determines the flavor of the wine is how well it has been fermented.

That flavor can be anywhere between two extremes: apple and butter. The more malolactic fermentation undergone by the grapes, the more prominent the apple flavor.

The more malic acid produced during fermentation, the more buttery the flavor.

When the oak of the grapevine is charred, the resultant wine has a sprinkle of toasty flavor to it. The oak being an active component of the overall flavor, Chardonnays are open to a much broader range of possibilities.

The region, climate, processing facility, and amount of charring can all contribute to the end flavor. This range includes the likes of coconut, spices, smoke, cream, caramel, and vanilla.

Additionally, the colder the grapes are when fermented, the fruitier the wine. Mango and pineapple are two reported flavors.

It’s no surprise that given Chardonnay’s wide range of flavors, it is among the most difficult to recognize in a blind taste test. Not many people are acquainted with the many flavors and blends Chardonnay can assume.

Merlot

Merlot is also a product of the Vitis vinifera grape. If the name wasn’t a dead giveaway (many people pronounce it mur-lot instead of mur-low), this is a wine with origins in France, specifically the Bordeaux – meaning “many thrushes” – grape species.

Another source of merlots is a speculated mutant grape found in Biturica, but there is no wide consensus on this. The drink goes down softly and is fairly sweet.

An extremely popular red wine, Merlot is produced all across the globe, but primarily in the romantic European countries.

Wine Production

The table below lists the top 10 wine producing countries. Measures represent the average annual tonnage of wine produced by the country.

1. France – 5.3 million
2. Italy – 4.7 million
3. Spain – 3.6 million
4. United States – 2.2 million
5. Argentina – 1.5 million
6. Australia – 1.4 million
7. China – 1.4 million
8. South Africa – 1.4 million
9. Chile – 977,000
10. Germany 890,000

From this data, it can be inferred that the best climate for wine is at least fifty degrees from the equator. Also take note that the top producers of wine are neo-Latin European countries.

Uses of Wine

You're probably surprised to see a section titled "Uses of Wine." And you're probably wondering what uses wine has besides drinking. Truth be told, there aren't many, but the purpose for drinking can be vastly different between individuals. Some people drink wine to be drunk, and some drink it as a sign of class. It may also be used for cooking and religious ceremonies.

Many deserts, such as the Black Forest Cherry, contain trace amounts of wine. Steaks, if you didn't know, are often marinated in wine before being cooked.

Probably the largest non-conventional use of wine is as a proponent of religious ceremonies. Due to its entheogen content, wine is a psychoactive substance, stimulating meditative states when used in moderation.

The Jewish Kiddush blessing prides itself on the consumption of wine.

In Christian teachings, the first miracle Jesus performed was transmuting water into wine, and wine is part of sacrament at many churches (although indistinguishable juice may be used as a substitute).On the other hand, Islamic law forbids wine. All alcohol is strictly forbidden in many Middle Eastern countries after the Islamic Revolution of 1979.

Wine has also been proposed to have a number of health benefits, though these extend only to red wine.

However, the legitimacy of these claims is in constant debate, and there's no consensus on whether or not the beverage can actually preserve your cardiovascular system, extend your life, or prevent the aging process.

Other claims about the health benefits of wine include maintaining heart health as well as resistance to disease when limited to one glass daily.

Sulphites are sometimes added to wine to help control the duration of fermentation or to help preserve the drink. In some instances, they have been known to cause respiratory problems.

On the contrary, excessive drinking, as with any other alcoholic beverage, can lead to serious liver damage as well as alcoholism.

Always be wary of the alcohol content in every wine you choose to drink.

They are not all made with the same amount of alcohol; therefore you should gauge yourself as not to induce any of the harmful effects.

Glassware

Finding the Right Glass

The type of wine glass you use depends on the type of wine you intend to drink from it. For red wines, the best choice is a wide glass. The common shape resembles a bowl.

These glasses allow adequate room to effectively swirl the wine. The recommended size for once of these glasses in anywhere between 10 to 20 ounces. This allows the most effective use.

For white wine, you should go in the complete opposite direction. The glass should be slender and a little bit taller than the red wine glass.

Even though the glass is taller than the red wine one, is should only hold about half as much fluid.

How to Hold Your Glass

The easiest way to determine how much experience someone has with wine is to watch the way they hold and drink from their glass. The proper technique is also important to etiquette when engaged with high-class company. You should always hold your glass by the stem with your palm cupping the bottom of the bowl.

Avoid grasping the glass by the bowl because the heat from your body will rapidly warm the wine, making the concoction undrinkable by many standards. This also prevents fingerprints and other grime from staining the glass.

Washing Wine Glasses

The biggest difficulty in washing glasses is removing the residue at the very bottom of the glass, especially with white wine glasses.

Obviously, you want to clean all of the wine from the glass to prevent unwanted mixtures during your next use as well as staining. Rinsing with hot water can help to “loosen” dry wine.

Use a minimal amount of dish soap, and be sure to rinse all of the soap from the glass before setting it out to dry. You may need a sponge to maneuver to the bottom of white wine glasses.

If you prefer to use a dishwasher to handle your dishes, understand that glasses with longer stems are prone to break. Only wash them in the dishwasher if you must; otherwise, stick with hand washing. Even if you do use a dishwasher, be sure to look over the dishes before they completely dry because there might still be wine that never washed out completely. If so, wash them out, then leave them out to air dry.

The Methodology of Wine Tasting

Established Hierarchy

At a respectable wine tasting party, elders should always be served before the younger, and women should be served before the men.

It's up to the host to decide the cutoff age for the elder group. As the host of the party, it is your responsibility to ensure that everyone has tasted the wine before you drink your share.

There's also a methodology to deciding which wines you taste first. Wines should be served in ascending order according to the strength of their flavors.

Stronger flavors will leave impressions on your tongue that distract from your ability to taste other wines. For this reason, it might also be a good idea to serve everyone water to drink in between wines.

As far as types of wines are concerned, they should be administered in the following order: sparkling, light white, heavy white, roses, light red, heavy red, then sweet.

If you are presenting wine that none of the participants have tasted, decide its order based on its color and any descriptors on its label.

However, it is advised that you know the strength of the wines beforehand unless you're having a blind tasting party.

Assessing Characteristics

There are also manual techniques for discovering the qualities of wine. Within a margin of error, the sweetness or heaviness of a wine can be determined by the swirling method.

Sweet or heavy red wines leave swirls or little rings on the glass, commonly referred to as "legs." The wider the bowl of your glass, the easier it is to produce and identify these rings, which means you can more accurately assess the sweetness and heaviness of the wine.

Most wines have a variety of characteristics used to pinpoint exactly what they are, and it takes years of training to become precise. Varietal wines are thick in the scent of the compositional grapes.

Practiced tasters can differentiate between various blends simply by smelling the wine.

Another factor that can be used to determine what kind of wine you're drinking is integration. Integration refers to the summated properties of acid content, tannin, and alcohol content, among others.

Some producers think it's best to have these properties all in balance, but others believe that skewing the ratio can create more distinct flavors.

The final quality of wine is expressiveness, described as the ability of the wine to portray its determined characteristics through its flavor.

The better the taste matches the ingredients, the more expressive that wine is considered.

Ranks of Wine

While it is acceptable to make slight variations, there is a standard system to calculate numerical ranks. Standardization allows for a hassle-free determination of which wines are deemed more impressive than others. When scoring, a wine should be broken down into its constituent parts. These can include, but are not limited to, smell (or nose), palate (or taste), and the expressiveness.

Make sure that all participants are aware of the established system of scoring before beginning.

Even two systems that score the same characteristics may not produce the results due to a weighted system. Some qualities of the wine may be considered more important than others.

For example, expressiveness might contribute to 65% of the score and appearance might be 10%.

In this case, scoring a 10 in appearance may not be as good as scoring a 5 in expressiveness.

Wine Tasting Etiquette

Given the consideration that it is a high-class event, there are several formalities to be observed when hosting a wine tasting party. That doesn't imply that the rules may be different elsewhere – wine tasting etiquette is always the same, regardless where you are.

The second consideration is to invite no more people to a venue than can be comfortably seated. The reasoning behind this is obvious.

Everyone needs some degree of personal space to feel at ease. Large audiences can also inflict pressure on participants. They'll rush through tasting the wine and have poor judgment as a result.

Wherever you decide to hold the tasting party, make sure there is an ample amount of water to go around.

This procedure is explained through two necessities: the necessity to purge the taste of one wine before trying the next and the necessity to prevent drunkenness during the course of consuming a potentially large amount of alcohol. If there is none present, chances are your guests will request some.

Similar to keeping water handy, you should also maintain a steady supply of hors d'oeuvres.

These should be generally unflavored snacks (no fruit snacks) such as white bread. This also works to prevent drunkenness, and the plain taste won't affect that of the wine.

Decanting

With some wines, it is sometimes necessary to decant before serving. Whether or not it disrupts or enhances the taste (or perhaps corrects) – and if that modification leaves room for fair review, is widely debated among enthusiasts.

When one decants wine, they do so with the sole purpose of removing settled sediments that haven't dissolved into the solution, but the high surface area exposure of the wine to oxygen during this process is thought to negatively impact the wine even if the goal of decanting does improve it in some amount.

Blind Tasting

Blind tasting is the preferred method of holding wine tasting ceremonies. Because it seeks to eliminate any way of identifying a wine before it's drunk, the possibility of bias is also eliminated. Those who have extensive experience with wine eventually learn to differentiate wine types simply based on the shape and size of a bottle, and most everyone can tell significant differences based on the color of the wine.

One way to reduce this bias is to serve wines in translucent glasses. Of course, someone has to pour the wines initially. That responsibility must always be delegated to the host.

Since he likely purchased all of the wine – or at least stored it – he cannot accrue any more bias than he already has, and the ratings of the numerous other participants can effectively counterbalance the bias of a single member.

You can also remove or replace the labels on your bottles or place your bottles in sleeves. It's surprising how much bias can arise from seemingly simple factors such as price, reputation, color, and the vineyard where the grapes were obtained and fermented.

Vertical Tasting

During vertical tasting, the goal is to access the change over time of one wine variety as opposed to comparing several different varieties.

For example, you may have one bottle of wine variety A from each year from 2000-2006. More important than the change between years is the consistency because it is a direct indication of the way the winery prepares their product, something like a watermark. As opposed to blind tasting, it is absolutely essential that all of the participants know exactly what wine they're drinking and when.

Horizontal Tasting

Horizontal tasting is very similar to its vertical cousin. As with the last, you must serve the same variety of wine each time.

However, they must all be from the same year and different producers. For a given year, you can determine which winery produced the better product. Of course, the sample size isn't large enough to make any generalizations.

Wine Acclimation

Most participants in a tasting party will have likely already tried this. If not, it should be their first tasting. The most proper name for it is a "tasting flight" during which a large number of different wines are lined up on a table, coupled with index cards that describe their properties. The goal is for the tasters to get an idea about how the physical properties all contribute to the overall taste of the wine.

Once one has participated in a tasting flight, other tasting parties will be much more interesting.

Old Versus New Tasting

This activity is a comparison between wine in the first countries to ferment it and the countries to later ferment it. The Old World line of wine producers is primarily the Latin countries of France, Spain, and Italy, among others. The New World consists mostly of continents with a boundary on the Pacific Ocean.

Because wine has been in production for so long now, Old vs New encompasses less of a comparison between the quality of the wines, but rather a deep look into the technique used in creating the wines from the two areas.

Mixed Tasting

Many people enjoy putting two or three different tasting events together. Imagine blind tasting while looking to differentiate between Old World and New World wines.

The complexity and depth of mixed wine tastes is what makes them so appealing to experienced wine enthusiasts. The combinations are quite numerous, so there's no shortage of ways to make your wine tasting interesting.

Tasting Wine with Cheese

Oftentimes, wine is also tasted to measure its compatibility with other foods. One of the most popular food choices to be consumed with wine is cheese, a dairy product that can vastly alter the distinct taste of your wine.

For example, it is accepted that Cabernet sauvignon is best served with a side of blue cheese. This may or may not be prepared alongside bread.

The effect of blue cheese on wine is that of calming. It forms a thin film on your tongue and mouth that not only helps the wine go down smoother, but adds an extra dimension of flavor.

Measure the difference between plain wine and wine with cheese by first drinking the wine plain.

You may want to rinse your mouth afterwards. Then, eat the cheese and quickly follow it with another serving of wine.

Tasting Wine with Chocolate

Quite a surprising pick, chocolate also makes for a competent compliment to wine, but only if mixed correctly. Many report having a bitter or sour taste in their mouth when drinking wine after chocolate. This is likely due to low compatibility between that specific wine and that specific chocolate. For best results, they should have roughly the same sweetness.

As a rule of thumb, lighter wines are most appropriate to drink with white chocolate and darker or redder wines best mix with dark chocolate. Before serving wine and chocolate en masse, make sure that your selected chocolates match the taste of corresponding wines.

Blind Price Tasting

Priceless wine tasting is withholding the cost of served wine until after they have all been drank. This measure insures that there's no price bias, the tendency to rate wines of higher value with better scores than those of lower value, regardless of actual taste.

Brand name recognition should also be avoided because many people associate brands and prices.

During an informal wine tasting, if everyone is expected to make a contribution towards the cost of wine, this can be resolved at the end of the event.

Price Point Tasting

This is similar to priceless tasting in that the prices of the wines are withheld, but the wines should all be within the same price range. This is a good way to cast doubt on the generalization that brand names and price aren't the ultimate factor in predetermining the quality of wine.

Big 8 Tasting

Big 8 is another derivative tasting that branches off of the tasting flight. Included beverages originate from both red and white wines, but only the four most prestigious from each group are considered.

From the red wines, you have the Cabernet Sauvignon, Pinot Noir, Shiraz, and Merlot. From the white wines, you have the Chardonnay, Riesling, Pinot, and Sauvignon Blanc. For inexperienced tasters just getting a hold on the varieties of wines – just like with the expanding tasting flight – a Big 8 tasting helps you to familiarize yourself with the qualities of wines.

This is not a recommended activity for advanced tasters as they'll be more or less treading the same ground. However, occasional informal Big 8 tastings can help to reestablish basic boundaries after long periods of more advance tasting proceedings.

Considerations During Tasting

We've already discussed that there are certain aspect of wine that you want to be looking for when tasting. The hard part is recognizing them all as quickly as possible, with as few glasses as possible.

The first step is noting the color of the wine, a feature apparent after pouring. Also take note of the clarity which can be done by tilting the glass and observing it from various angles.

Color is most easily visible when the glass is surrounded by white. Colored materials etc. are of troubling color, hold up a napkin to the glass to help filter out some of those reflections.

Though there is an infinite range of possible colors of wine, there are standards that you should be on the lookout for. For red wines, these are purple, maroon, ruby, garnet, brick, or beige.

For white wines, look for pale yellow, green, golden, amber, or light brown. As you become more adept, you'll be capable of linking these colors to several other attributes.

While you're swirling the glass to assess pigmentation, also search the bottom of the glass for the presence of sediment. The third property that can be determined by swirling or plainly observing the wine is how much luster the wine has.

Is it dull or cloudy? Is it plain or does it have a sparkle to it? These aspects also go a long way to practiced connoisseurs. Lastly, swirling the wine will help to vaporize some of the alcohol, which also happens to release some of its aroma. Take this moment to grace yourself with a deep inhale of the aroma. This, too, has a particular form that should be adhered to.

Your nose should be as close to the wine as possible without actually touching it which may be considered rude by the host. Try to relate the smell of the wine with other scents you are familiar with. Common comparisons are berries, flowers, oaks, and more.

Swirling the wine allows you to smell the natural and true aromas of the wine. The more wines you sniff and drink, the easier it will be for you to instantaneously relate the aroma to the quality of the wine.

This is something that is better experienced than explained.

The coveted next step is actually tasting the wine. Begin with a small and gentle sip. Caress the fluid with your tongue and let it momentarily drift in your mouth.

It is during this important step that you're measuring the core characteristics of the wine: alcohol content, acidity, sweetness, etc. Formulate a first impression, a lasting impression, and a final impression.

What you should be considering at this moment is how well the qualities of the wine are balanced. Which components stick out the most to you, and which are most subtle? More importantly, how do those features contribute to the overall expression of the wine?

After your first sip has been absolved from your mouth, move into the middle range phase which is where the bulk of your review should be derived.

Generate a "flavor profile" based on your experience. What is the general flavor? How long does the flavor reside in your mouth? Lastly, does it have an aftertaste, and what is it?

Initially bitter wines can later be sweet and vice versa. All of these together will let you know how you truly feel about the wine.

How to Host a Wine Tasting Party

With most of this book behind you, you are now prepared to host a fun social event.

First time wine tasters may not enjoy themselves as much as seasoned participants because everything will be so unfamiliar to them, but through learning, everyone involved will come to have a great time.

Before inviting all of your friends over, decide what kind of tasting you'll be hosting.

If this is your absolute first time, it's best to go for a Big 8 so that your friends, who are likely inexperienced, can get the basic foundation they need to participate in some of the more advanced events. Whether or not to present side dishes such as cheese is completely up to you.

Now you can move on to compiling the list of guests. Getting started, you should try to make up a list of people you believe will be genuinely interested, and remember that everyone you invite likely won't show up. For your maximum expected company, make sure you have enough seats and enough space to house everyone comfortably.

Typically, the more room you have, the more people you can invite without your guests feeling cluttered or rushed to drink.

The number of guests you invite also directly affects how much wine you'll need – an expense you'll have to pay up front. There should be enough wine for everyone to get a taste of every available drink.

When inviting friends over, try to limit the guest list to a group of individuals who all have roughly the same amount of experience in tasting wine.

A group of experienced tasters with a small amount of novices will make things slow and uninteresting for the majority; the opposite will make the event boring for the minority. Either invite all beginners, all intermediate, or all experts.

Design cards for each guest. Every guest should have a card for every wine, and the cards should have space for guests to record their observations when drinking their wine.

Also be sure to include a designated space on the cards for recording scores. This will make things much easier when tallying numbers at the end of the pleasantries.

Decorations are typically important in helping to establish the right mood, but don't worry yourself too much with this aspect. If you don't have time for it, don't worry.

However, you should always find time to place a cloth over the table that you'll be drinking the wine on. It might be hard to go an entire evening without anything spilling, and you don't want to have to disrupt the flow of the event to clean up or to deal with permanent stains on your furnishings.

If you can manage more than a cloth, flowers are always a nice addition as well as dim candles for mood and wine-related paintings.

If you do decide to have candles, keep them primarily in areas of the house where you don't expect to be tasting wine. The room you use needs to be well lit to circumvent any difficulty in properly determining the color or cloudiness of the wine. Having multiple sources of light provides a source of error from the multiple reflections.

Remember to serve the driest wines first and make your way up to the sweeter ones. When you do begin tasting the sweet wines, make sure there is water available to help neutralize any flavor left on your guests' tongues after the tasting.

In addition to that, there are several other considerations to be made. First, drink wines according to color – light to dark. Second, drink wine according to age – youngest to oldest. These regulations all help to maintain balance during the tasting party.

Limit the amount of wine you pour for each of your guests. Two ounces is usually enough for them to properly taste without being overabundant.

At the end of the day, you always want to have wine left over. It is your choice whether you want to keep the wine for yourself or let each of your guests take a bottle of choice home with them.

Even if you don't serve your wine with cheese or chocolate, you should always have enough unflavored snacks and water for the reasons explained beforehand.

Besides, drinking all of that wine, your guests are likely to get sick of it without anything else to stimulate their sense of taste.

The absolute most important consideration is ensuring that all of your guests get home safely. After the amount of drinking likely to occur by each of the members, it's doubtful that anyone won't be under the influence to a noticeable degree.

This might mean that, when inviting guests, you may wish to look into finding people who will attend the tasting party but not drink, people who can act as designated drivers. If it is convenient in your location, paying for taxis is a generous notion.

As the host, personally delivering some of your intoxicated friends to their homes (with the assumption that you haven't participated) is the most responsible course of action. The best precaution is to let no one participate if they can't confirm with you the availability of their ride home.

Wine Ratings

Like everything else in the material world, wines are the target of a system of rating that seeks to numerically categorize them based on quality. Unlike many things, the highest rating for a wine is six as opposed to five.

Again unlike other things, wine rating can be reliably performed by anyone so long as they've had prolonged exposure to the culture of wine production and tasting. Their analysis should center around the four primary aspects of wine: aroma, appearance, taste, and aftertaste.

Any star that is able to average six stars from a wide sample of raters is believed to be near perfect. The amount of praise allocated to these wines is well-deserved as not even one percent of all wines produced all around the world have managed to achieve the rating.

These classic concoctions have a complex blend of characteristics intentionally manipulated by the production company. Finding these wines in stores or online is also near impossible – the majority of them sit as collectors' items in the homes of enthusiasts.

Five-star wines are still extremely good varieties. From color to consistency to viscosity, their almost as good as their six-star brothers.

The smell and taste are also above par, but they tend to be missing the extra kick found in six-starred products. Even four-star wines are fairly impressive, comprising the top five percent of all wines produced. What tends to make them sit below five-star wines is that they're too young to have developed strong, distinctive tastes.

You generally don't run into average or mediocre wines until three stars. They tend to be "cliché" in a way, their flavor too ordinary to be considered for higher ratings.

These average wines are where production flaws begin to stick out as well. This isn't to say they aren't good wines; they simply would be more appropriate for casual events rather than formal ones.

Wines that fail to accrue three stars fail to leave a good impression on tasters. They are often either bland or taste poor, most often as a result of being fermented from less-than-standard materials.

Input has a large role to play in a resultant wine, so you can assume that these two-star wines lack complexity as a result of the cheapness of their producers.

By the time you get down to one-star wines, it's clear that no respectable wine enthusiast would be found taking a second sip of the product. A majority of these wines are homemade concoctions that were either improperly fermented, made from second-rate materials, or both.

The goal of wine tasting and the subsequent rating is to create a standardized system for those who can appreciate the generally overlooked qualities of wine.

To this end, most procedures are carried out in large groups. Tasted wines must be served with absolutely no knowledge of their identities. At the end of such a session, ballots are collected and sorted.

Once a large enough volume of responses has been produced for a wine, the final score is determined and published. Serious wine drinkers rely heavily on these ratings to determine which products they wish to consume both for leisure and for special events such as wine tasting parties. Like everything else, some raters value some qualities more than they do others, and this is increasingly important to consumers, especially when they have their own preferences. At the end of the day, it's your decision.

How to Serve Wine

It's finally time to pop the cork on that prized bottle of wine you've been saving. Whether for a college graduation, consummating a marriage, the birth of a child, or a simple reunion of familiar faces, knowing how to professionally prepare and serve wine will make the experience that much more memorable.

Making the most out of any wine is a delicate process. Everything from selecting, chilling, opening, and finally serving require special considerations.

Keeping these in mind will be a great service to your guests.

The taste of wine – most alcoholic beverages, actually – depends on the temperature it is stored at before serving.

Different types of wine have different requirements. All white wines should be chilled, simply accomplished by leaving them in your refrigerator as soon as possible after purchasing.

You want its temperature to drop to roughly fifty-five degrees Fahrenheit, and you want to maintain that temperature as much as possible. White wines are served this way to control their typically high levels of acidity. If you are too pressed for time for the fridge to do the trick, fill a bucket with ice water and allow the drink to sit in the mixture.

Red wines are more sensitive to drops in temperature. You want to serve them at room temperature, so avoid using a refrigerator to chill them.

Sudden changes in temperature can degrade the taste, so try to find a room that is around sixty-five to seventy degrees to leave it in.

Altering your air conditioning is a viable method of temperature control. It is okay to also serve red wines slightly chilled, in which case you'll need to exert quite a bit of work to ensure the temperature doesn't drop far below sixty.

Should you happen to chill a red wine for too much, the best solution is to let it sit out at room temperature.

As said, any changes in temperature that are too sudden will alter the condition of the wine, likely for the worse. If you are pressed for time, an adequately distanced heater also helps to remedy the situation.

Only when your guests are ready to consume the wine should you remove them from their storage. When you do get to that point, your first course of action is to remove to foil. Try to be neat as to avoid pieces of the foil falling into the bottle. With an all-purpose corkscrew, removal should be simple.

Without spending too much time on it, remove as much of the foil as possible. With that obstruction out of the way, you can begin removing the cork.

In the unfortunate situation that pieces of the foil or cork fall into the bottle, take quick action. Pour the wine into a decanter, coffee filter, or any other appropriate device for straining. When you're done, pour the wine back into its proper bottle.

If removing the cork from a "sparkling" drink, additional precautions will be necessary. You won't need a corkscrew for this; rather, use your thumb to wedge the cork free. You should have the bottle pointed away from guests and only open it if it hasn't been recently shaken.

If there's too much pressure built up in the bottle, the wine will shoot from the bottle when the cork is removed.

The properties of the glass you use to serve the wine should be as follows: a long stem (handle) with a wide bowl that narrows as it moves to the top. The wide shape makes swirling the wine much more effective.

The narrowed top strengthens the density of the fragrance as it escapes the glass. The long stem allows you plenty of space to hold the glass so that your hands around the bowl don't cause sudden increases in the wine's temperature.

Surprisingly, this variety of glass is acceptable for both red and white wines. You can opt to use thinner glasses for white wines if you so desire, but the sheer number of glasses may cause unwanted clutter if serving a large number of people.

There have been advancements in accepted styles of wine glasses, the newest variety having an incredibly short stem with no room to grip.

Instead, they simply stand on a foot that supports the bowl with nothing but several centimeters of stem. These glasses have two major drawbacks.

The first is that they are highly susceptible to stains, and the second is that your forced grip on the bowl causes unwarranted heating of the wine.

Poured wine should only reach about halfway up the glass. The abundance of extra space considers the need to swirl the wine. Always serve lighter colored wines before darker colors and younger wines before older ones. This order of drinking was established so that stronger flavors are tasted last; weaker flavors have smaller chances of making an impression of the taste of the next drink.

Serving Wine – Quick Tips

Procedure for Opening Wine

When wines are bottled, the neck is sealed by an airtight cork. Opening wine consists of removing this cork. Beginners should show extreme caution as to prevent pieces of the cork from falling into the wine.

The only way to remove these is by pouring, and guests will be disgusted to have it in their glass. Familiarize yourself with the corkscrew you use before opening wines you plan on publically serving.

For best results, insert the corkscrew directly in the middle of the cork. When it is as far in as you can get it, begin to turn the mechanism at the top of the screw which will drill the screw into the cork.

As you do this, the arms of the corkscrew will rise. Lastly, once the screw has been completely inserted, push down on the two arms simultaneously. This will release the cork.

Properly Storing Wine

Different wines have particular circumstances under which they can thrive. Some are best left at room temperature and others are best refrigerated.

Those that need special attention will typically say so somewhere on the label. “Serve chilled” and “refrigerate before opening” are two good examples of this. Serving wine at the wrong temperature can drastically alter its intended taste.

If there are no self-descript labels explaining preparation for a wine, there are general guidelines you can resort to.

White Wines: 45 to 50 degrees

Sparkling Wines: 41 to 51 degrees

Rose Wines: 45 to 55 degrees

Red wines: 50 to 64 degrees

Fortified Wines: 54 to 65 degrees

How to Chill Wine

When pressed for time, the only real substitute for chilling wine is giving it a few minutes in the freezer. However, the result is not the same. Proper chilling should occur for an extended duration with the wine placed in a bucket of ice water. If you don’t include water, the surface area of convection won’t be large enough to properly chill the wine.

For a bucket intended for a single wine bottle, fill it halfway with ice and add water until seventy-five percent of the bucket is filled. Submerge the bottle in this mixture for forty-five minutes, give or take.

If you store your wine in the refrigerator, it may take up to several hours to get the correct temperature, but it's more economic if you have the time.

Over-chilling wine can also degrade the taste. The product should be a "refreshing" cold, not "ice-cold."

If the drink is too cold, you'll have to sit it out to warm, and both the change in temperature and the oxygen exposure can affect the taste.

Preserving Opened Wine

Before storing leftover wine anywhere, replace the cork. Despite some superstitions, it is okay to keep your wine stored in a refrigerator.

However, the more you move the wine between room temperature and refrigeration, the lower its quality will be. Only remove it when you plan on drinking a good bit. Still, it is best to have a cellar-esque area set forth for the most practical and efficient storage of your excess wines. Low temperatures in moist environments are ideal.

The absolute worst place to store your wine is on top of your refrigerator. If you've ever put an arm or hand close to the top or back of your fridge, you should have noticed it was fairly hot. This is a horrible climate for the preservation of your alcohol.

For long term storage (up to and over six Months), then it becomes increasingly important that your preferred area is dark, highly humid, and as cold as necessary.

Oxidation of Wine

Oxidation occurs when wine is exposed to oxygen for prolonged periods of time. Signs of oxidation are clear, but are sometimes only apparent after drinking the wine.

They include discoloration, foul odor, and a brownish tint. If you're unlucky enough to forego having these qualities in your wine, the flavor of oxidized wine is enough to give away that it shouldn't be drank.

The most common reasons wine becomes oxidized is because it's not properly sealed. Both when you buy wine and reapply a cork after opening, make sure the cork is tight and secure in the neck of the bottle.

Serving oxidized wine to your guests is among one of the most embarrassing experiences a host can have a wine tasting party. It likely won't make any of your guests sick, but it will provide them with a memorable but awful experience with wine.

Conclusion

As simple as it may sound, there are many considerations to make before you can be sure your wine tasting party will successfully cater to the level of expertise of your guests as well as offer an environment where everyone can be comfortable and wine that lives up to the expectations of its producers.

Having reached the end of this book, you should be fully aware of all the proper procedures for embarking on this high-class event.

Nonetheless, if this is your first wine tasting party, don't hesitate to consult other sources and study up on wine in general before proclaiming yourself the host of this fun event.

Also, don't be a blind host. You should have an idea about the different varieties of wines and their attributes before you host a party.

The guest should be able to learn something from you. You might even want to consider being a guest at another host's party before throwing your own.

With technical knowledge and that of proper etiquette in hand, it's time to lay down the rules of the game, scour through your contacts, and assemble your wine tasting party!

www.ingramcontent.com/pod-product-compliance
Ingram Content Group UK Ltd.
Pitfield, Milton Keynes, MK11 3LW, UK
UKHW041840200726
13854UKWH00003BA/1238

9 781304 710857